D0554879

CALIFORNIA
MISSIONS

Discovering Mission San Francisco Solano

BY OSCAR CANTILLO

Cavendish
Square

New York

Published in 2015 by Cavendish Square Publishing, LLC
243 5th Avenue, Suite 136, New York, NY 10016

Copyright © 2015 by Cavendish Square Publishing, LLC

First Edition

No part of this publication may be reproduced, stored in a retrieval system, or transmitted in any form or by any means—electronic, mechanical, photocopying, recording, or otherwise—without the prior permission of the copyright owner. Request for permission should be addressed to Permissions, Cavendish Square Publishing, 243 5th Avenue, Suite 136, New York, NY 10016. Tel (877) 980-4450; fax (877) 980-4454.

Website: cavendishsq.com

This publication represents the opinions and views of the author based on his or her personal experience, knowledge, and research. The information in this book serves as a general guide only. The author and publisher have used their best efforts in preparing this book and disclaim liability rising directly or indirectly from the use and application of this book.

CPSIA Compliance Information: Batch #WS14CSQ

All websites were available and accurate when this book was sent to press.

Library of Congress Cataloging-in-Publication Data

Cantillo, Oscar.
Discovering Mission San Francisco Solano / Oscar Cantillo.
pages cm. — (California Missions)
Includes index.
ISBN 978-1-62713-055-4 (hardcover) ISBN 978-1-62713-057-8 (ebook)
1. Mission San Francisco Solano (Sonoma, Calif.)—History—Juvenile literature. I. Title.

F869.M654C36 2015
979.4'18—dc23

2014003729

Editorial Director: Dean Miller
Editor: Kristen Susienka
Copy Editor: Cynthia Roby
Art Director: Jeffrey Talbot
Designer: Douglas Brooks
Photo Researcher: J8 Media
Production Manager: Jennifer Ryder-Talbot
Production Editor: David McNamara

The photographs in this book are used by permission and through the courtesy of: Cover photo by Ambient Images Inc./SuperStock; Pixtal/SuperStock, 1; Ambient Images Inc./SuperStock, 4; © Universal Images Group Limited/Alamy, 7; Pomo Indians gather acorns for winter storage in hivelike granaries (colour litho), Kihn, William Langdon (1898-1957)/National Geographic Creative/The Bridgeman Art Library, 8–9; © North Wind/North Wind Picture Archives, 12; © 2014 Pentacle Press, 13; © North Wind/North Wind Picture Archives, 15; In Collection of California Missions Resource Center, 18; National Geographic/Getty Images, 20; Courtesy CMRC, 22; Courtesy of UC Berkeley, Bancroft Library, 24–25; © Pentacle Press, 26; Pierce C.C. (Charles C.)/File:Painting of Fort Vallejo and Mission San Francisco Solano de Sonoma, ca.1900 (CHS-1910).jpg/Wikimedia Commons, 30–31; © North Wind Picture Archives/The Image Works, 33; © ZUMA Press, Inc./Alamy, 34; Pixtal/SuperStock, 41.

Printed in the United States of America

CALIFORNIA
MISSIONS

Contents

San Francisco Solano in Sonoma, California, was the last mission in the Spanish mission chain.

1
The Spanish Empire in the New World

THE SONOMA VALLEY

The Valley of the Moon, located in Sonoma, California, is known for its majestic beauty and rich history. Today, Sonoma is at the heart of the wine industry, surrounded by rolling hills and vineyards. But its history is vast, filled with opportunity and conquests. Within this history is the story of Mission San Francisco Solano. To understand this mission and its purpose, however, one must first know how it came to be.

THE SPANISH REACH CALIFORNIA

Working on behalf of the Spanish king and queen Ferdinand and Isabella, Italian explorer Christopher Columbus sailed to what was known as the New World (North America, South America, and Central America) in 1492. On Columbus' return to Spain, he bore exotic objects and food, and people from lands unknown, which led the Spaniards to uphold him as a hero. Spain then wanted to own more of the world.

In 1519, shortly after Columbus published a map of his sea route, experienced soldier and explorer Hernán Cortés used it to guide his journey. He arrived in what is known today as Mexico. His intent was to claim the land for Spain. On arrival, he and his soldiers encountered the powerful Aztec empire, which they conquered in 1521. Cortés named the country New Spain and set up a government there. The ruler of that government held the position of **viceroy**, a person who acts in place of the king. In 1542, the viceroy sent explorer Juan Rodríguez Cabrillo by boat to claim the lands north of New Spain, those known today as the Baja Peninsula, California, and the West Coast. Because Cabrillo's and others' searches failed to uncover rare or desired items, such as gold, no further explorations took place after 1602.

It was not until the mid-1700s that King Carlos III, feeling threatened by the rumor that Russians had landed in Alta California, sent Spanish **friars**, often called *frays*, along with soldiers to explore the area once more. The friars and soldiers were tasked to set up **Franciscan** missions around California to educate the indigenous, or Native, people and teach them the ways of **Christianity**, as well as resettle the area for Spain. About a day's ride stood between each of the twenty-one missions—a road dubbed *El Camino Real*, meaning "the royal road" in Spanish, connected all.

MISSION SAN FRANCISCO SOLANO

The mission established in the Valley of the Moon was called Mission San Francisco Solano, the last of the twenty-one Franciscan missions in California.

2
The Coast Miwok and the Pomo

THE NATIVE PEOPLE OF THE VALLEY OF THE MOON

The Spanish people brought the Coast Miwok and Pomo people to Mission San Francisco Solano. Before then, they had lived on the lands—the Coast Miwok on the peninsula across from San Francisco, and the Pomo farther north—between 3,500 and 5,000 years before the Spanish arrived. In terms of what they wore, how they constructed their homes, hunting techniques, and diet, the lifestyles of the two tribes were very similar. Before the Spanish came to the land, they coexisted relatively peacefully.

No one knows for sure where the tribes originated. However, some believe that

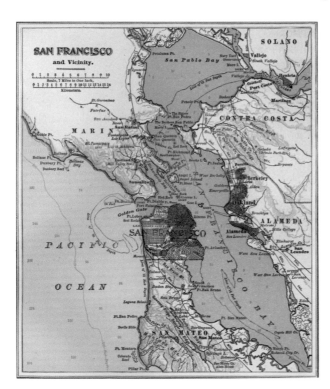

The area around San Francisco was rich with wildlife and was home to many Native people.

The Pomo collected acorns every year. They used them to make bread and other foods. Sometimes they stored them in man-made granaries for later use.

a few thousand years ago, the Miwok left the Ural Mountains in Siberia, which are located in the eastern part of Russia, and walked across the land that connected Alaska and Russia at that time. The tribes then traveled down the coast of what is now Canada and into Alta California.

HOW THEY HUNTED

Before the Spanish appeared and introduced farming, the Pomo and Coast Miwok were hunters and gatherers, meaning they did not grow crops or raise animals but instead used the plants, animals, and sea life around them for food. Acorns were especially important because they were widely available and a large part of peoples' diets. They were also easily stored for later use. Other

important food items included marine life, such as salmon, mussels, and oysters that flourished in the bays; and plants, such as mushrooms and roots

The indigenous people used the land without hurting it so it could support them forever. They did not cut down forests, kill entire animal populations, or create pollution. When droughts or rainy seasons destroyed certain types of plants, they moved to different areas or collected other foods. They were adaptable and interested in using only what they had earned.

HOW THEY LIVED

The women usually did the cooking, while the men hunted. During the day, aside from preparing food, both men and women spent some of the time making tools, such as arrowheads, spears, bowls, and musical instruments.

Both the Pomo and Miwok lived in settlements—communities of homes spread out across a certain area of land—or villages. The houses were often small, circular huts made from resources found within their environment. This included wood, bark, reeds, mud, and anything else they could find. Almost all houses had a fire pit and a hole in the roof to allow smoke from the fire to escape while cooking.

CLOTHING AND TRADITIONS

Men and women wore different types of clothing depending on the weather. During warmer seasons, women dressed in a simple skirt or apron, while men covered the lower parts of their bodies with deerskin. In colder months, both men and women wore the warm furs of animals.

Interestingly, the Miwok also decorated their bodies with tattoos and jewelry. They held a tradition of strapping a **cradleboard** to the backs of babies' heads to give them a flat shape, which they thought to be attractive.

TRADING AND RELIGIOUS PRACTICES

Trading was also important. The Pomo and Miwok often traded amongst themselves and with their neighbors. They also held their own religious practices, believing in maintaining balance between humans and nature. Many occasions, such as births, deaths, and marriages, were celebrated.

3
The Mission System

CLAIMING CALIFORNIA FOR THE SPANISH

In the mid-1700s, when Spain renewed its interest in Alta California, the reason was largely to claim the region for Spain before the Russians could claim it for themselves. For King Carlos III, founding the missions was an important first step in turning Alta California into a Spanish colony. He wanted the **missionaries** to **convert** the indigenous people in the area. He knew that if the Native people spoke Spanish, as well as considered themselves subjects of Spain, it would be harder for the Russians to move south and claim any of Alta California's land for Russia.

There were several noteworthy people in the history of the first missions, but perhaps one of the most important was Fray Junípero Serra.

FRAY SERRA'S JOURNEY

Born on the Spanish island of Majorca but having moved across the world at a young age, Fray Junípero Serra had lived in New Spain for almost twenty years by the time of the missions. There he taught Spanish, preached, and converted the people Native to

Fray Junípero Serra was the first leader of the Alta California missions.

the area. He was deeply devoted to introducing Christianity to the people of New Spain. Thus when King Carlos III, in 1769, sent an expedition to found the first mission in Alta California, one of the parties included Fray Serra. During his lifetime, Fray Serra founded nine of the missions and became the first president of the mission system.

BEGINNING THE MISSIONS

Fray Serra and his men arrived at the site of the first mission, San Diego de Alcalá, at the end of June 1769. It was an area rich in fresh water and timber and was inhabited by large numbers of Native people, who were at first suspicious of the friars. In fact, during the entire first year of its existence, not a single Native person converted to Christianity.

The friars were not discouraged by the lack of early converts. They knew that with the vast resources of the Spanish empire, particularly its military might, the Native people of Alta California would eventually become part of the mission system. With one mission in place, the system would expand over the years across 500 miles (805 km) of California coast, as far north as Mission San Francisco Solano.

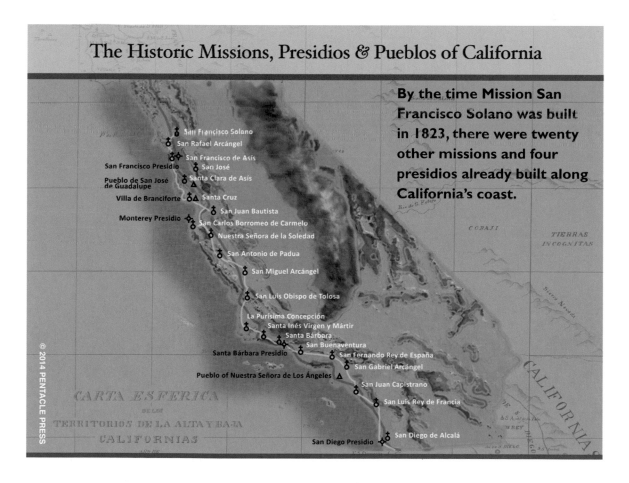

The Historic Missions, Presidios & Pueblos of California

By the time Mission San Francisco Solano was built in 1823, there were twenty other missions and four presidios already built along California's coast.

San Francisco Solano
San Rafael Arcángel
San Francisco de Asís
San Francisco Presidio
San José
Pueblo de San José de Guadalupe
Santa Clara de Asís
Villa de Branciforte
Santa Cruz
San Juan Bautista
Monterey Presidio
San Carlos Borromeo de Carmelo
Nuestra Señora de la Soledad
San Antonio de Padua
San Miguel Arcángel
San Luis Obispo de Tolosa
La Purísima Concepción
Santa Inés Virgen y Mártir
Santa Bárbara
San Buenaventura
Santa Bárbara Presidio
San Fernando Rey de España
San Gabriel Arcángel
Pueblo of Nuestra Señora de Los Ángeles
San Juan Capistrano
San Luis Rey de Francia
San Diego de Alcalá
San Diego Presidio

© 2014 PENTACLE PRESS

4
Founding the Mission

The story of how Fray José Altimira founded Mission San Francisco Solano in 1823 is interesting and filled with unexpected events.

TROUBLE AT THE MISSION

In the early nineteenth century, the Spanish mission system had expanded from San Diego to San Francisco. Native people still populated the land north of San Francisco. By this time, several Franciscan missions had also been set up along El Camino Real. In 1819, Fray José Altimira, the most important man in San Francisco Solano's history, sailed from Spain to join the friars at Mission San Francisco de Asís—also called Mission Dolores—located in San Francisco.

On arrival, it was clear to Fray Altimira that Mission Dolores was in terrible shape. The missionaries there couldn't grow much food themselves because of the cold and wet weather, and the condition of the soil around the mission was poor. To make matters worse, there were fewer people working there compared to other

Mission San Francisco Solano began in part because Mission San Francisco de Asís (shown in the hand-colored woodcut above) was not managing well.

missions boasting larger numbers of workers. Women and men were tasked with the same chores, even lifting heavy objects. Also, many **neophytes**—Native people who had converted to Christianity—were dying from diseases brought over by the Europeans, such as measles and tuberculosis. Many others left Mission Dolores for healthier, sunnier missions, causing numbers at the mission to further decline.

Fray Altimira decided to do something about the declining numbers. He wrote to the Mexican governor of Alta California, Don Luis Argüello, and told him that Mission Dolores was doing poorly. In this letter he suggested a solution: close the mission and let Fray Altimira take the neophytes and the supplies, and found a new mission farther north.

PLANNING A NEW MISSION

Governor Argüello liked the idea of establishing another northern settlement and granted Fray Altimira permission to build his mission. The additional settlement would help protect the northern part of Alta California from Russian influence, which was still a threat to Spain. By that time, Russians had moved farther south than the northern parts they had previously occupied, and had even established a Russian settlement and fort, called Fort Ross.

The Spanish believed that the Russians wanted to claim some part of the New World for Russia, and, as a result, they did not trust the Russians. The Russians, in response, wanted to protect themselves from any Spanish attack. They armed their fort with several cannons and other weapons, and always had it guarded. However, when Fray Altimira decided to found the new mission in the north, he did not consider the Russians. He only thought about the thousands of northern Native people he would convert to Christianity.

Even before Fray Altimira and the missionaries with him began their journey north, they faced a problem that almost meant canceling the start of Mission San Francisco Solano. Fray Altimira had consulted the governor about his plan, but he had not spoken to the president of the Franciscan missions, Fray José Señan, who was ill and nearing the end of his life. When Fray Señan learned of Fray Altimira's plan to start the mission, he became upset. He informed Governor Argüello that neither he nor Fray Altimira had any power to start or close a mission. Fortunately, Fray Altimira had help from another friar, Fray Vicente Sarría, who was soon to replace Fray Señan as president of the Franciscan missions. Fray Sarría convinced the dying friar to allow the founding of Mission San Francisco Solano as long as Mission Dolores remained open, too. Fray Señan agreed. This meant that Fray Altimira could not bring many neophytes and materials from Mission Dolores, but instead had to build a new population and find new supplies, which was a far more difficult task.

ESTABLISHING THE MISSION SITE

On June 25, 1823, Fray Altimira left San Francisco to find a site for his new mission. He searched for a place with good farmland, an abundant supply of water, and a large indigenous population. He traveled with twenty-four soldiers and several neophytes. They sailed across the San Francisco Bay and landed near San Rafael. They then walked north for ten days. They climbed hills covered with grass and flowers, hiked through thick forests, and crossed cold rushing creeks. In the evenings, they fried fresh fish and roasted bear meat. In early July, they stopped.

Fray Altimira surveyed the farmland, ideal for growing and harvesting grapes, and hundreds of freshwater springs in Sonoma. He decided that the location was ideal to establish the newest mission site for Spain. Scooping some soil by a stream and glancing at the heavens, Fray Altimira decided to name the new mission San Francisco Solano, after a missionary that had worked in South America, converting many natives of Peru to Christianity.

Mission San Francisco Solano was dedicated and built quickly. Within three years, all buildings were completed, crops were doing well, and Native people were learning about Spanish culture.

5
Constructing the Mission

BLESSING SAN FRANCISCO SOLANO

The Sonoma site of Mission San Francisco Solano was officially blessed on July 4, 1823, ten days before the feast day of the saint San Francisco Solano, for whom the mission was named. Fray Altimira's early-morning blessing was witnessed by the people who had journeyed with him from San Francisco—soldiers, neophytes, and other friars. The fray planted a cross in the earth that he had fashioned from a tree. The ceremony also included prayers, Bible readings, and hymns. To celebrate the launch of Mission San Francisco Solano, Spanish soldiers fired their guns.

BUILDING STARTS

On August 25, 1823, Fray Altimira and a small group of neophyte laborers began to build Mission San Francisco Solano at Sonoma with determination and enthusiasm. Twelve soldiers stood guard to protect them against any threats while they worked. The church was the first structure to be constructed, and was dedicated in 1824. Priests' quarters were completed in 1825, and the entire mission was finished in 1826.

The mission's general design consisted of long, square-shaped buildings that formed a **quadrangle**. The church was built in one corner of the quadrangle, and residences, workshops, a kitchen, and a storage area completed the square shape.

Surrounding the structures, a low, wooden building plastered inside and out with whitewashed mud was built. This served as living quarters for the neophytes. Next to the quarters, fields of crops and orchards were planted. There was also ample grazing land for their livestock, which included cattle and sheep.

For the soldiers, a series of *palizadas*, or fenced-in areas, were constructed from poles tied together with cowhide, coated with mud, and thatched—a type of roofing technique—with **tule**, a type of reed. For the friars, they built an **adobe** house roofed with tiles.

Adobe is sun-dried brick made from mud and straw. The Spanish Californians preferred to build with adobe because it remains cool in the summer and warm in the winter. Unlike wood, however, it needs to be shaped into bricks and hardened by the sun or in an oven before it can be used. Fray Altimira was known to be impatient. He decided to begin building the structure

Techniques used by the neophytes to make adobe bricks are still used today.

before the adobe bricks were hardened. As a result, two unroofed adobe structures fell apart during an unexpected rainstorm. Once the rain had passed, though, Fray Altimira immediately began to rebuild.

By the spring of 1824, the

mission boasted a new, whitewashed wooden church. Later that year, Fray Altimira held an official dedication day. Fray Sarría, now president of the twenty-one missions, was also present. He gifted Mission San Francisco Solano a painting of San Francisco Solano, the patron saint of their new mission. Fray Altimira hung the painting above the church altar to remind all who visited of the origins of the mission.

ITEMS FOR THE MISSION

The last mission unfortunately did not receive many donated items and decorative objects from other mission churches. Yet the Russians at nearby Fort Ross gave generously to Fray Altimira and his community. They sent vases, hammered brass basins, hand-carved bookstands, picture frames, candles, hand-woven linens, embroidered silk veils for the tabernacle, and Mass bells. It seemed that a positive relationship between the friars at Mission San Francisco Solano and the Russians had developed. Friars from Mission San Francisco de Asís (Mission Dolores), however, were also generous in donating. Their gifts included 3,000 sheep, sixty horses, fifty cows, forty oxen, and many farming tools.

EXPANDING THE MISSION

Over the years, Fray Altimira continued to expand the mission. A **granary** and new wooden buildings for the soldiers and their families were built, as well as several larger adobe buildings where the missionaries and neophytes studied and worked. One building measured 120 feet (37 m) in length and 30 feet (9 m) in width. It

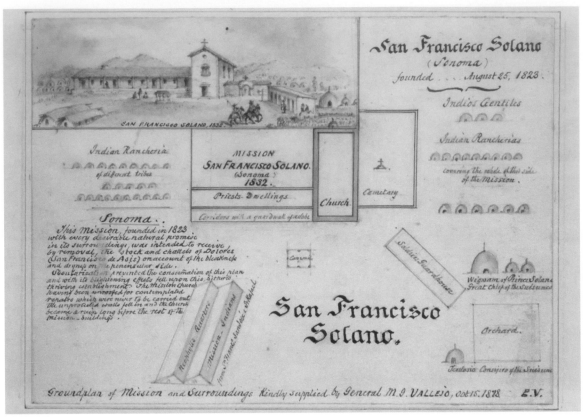

Mission San Francisco Solano had different areas for the church, the priests, and the neophytes, as well as orchards, farms, and a cemetery on its grounds, as depicted in the historic drawing above.

held a large corridor and a tiled roof. In 1825, the neophytes completed another wing of living quarters for the friars.

A new leader, Fray Buenaventura Fortuni, came to the mission in 1826. Under his guidance, many improvements were made to the mission, including the construction of a larger church, as well as a stone water cistern—a type of storage tank—that was located in the mission's courtyard. Until the cistern existed, residents of the mission had to walk to the river to fill buckets with water. Now fresh river water, perfect for drinking, washing, cooking, and laundry, was pumped right to the cistern.

Although the mission was nearing completion, there were several problems the people would face.

6
Life at the Mission

NATIVE PEOPLE AT THE MISSION

The mission began to increase in popularity. The friars preached to the Native people who lived nearby, and more were starting to listen. As a benefit, the friars offered the indigenous people regular meals and sleeping quarters. In return, the Native people worked in the fields and learned to be Christians. By 1830, almost 1,000 people were living at Mission San Francisco Solano, and most of its Native population had become neophytes.

The hunting-and-gathering life of the Pomo and Coast Miwok tribes changed from day to day and season to season. Mission life, however, was exactly the same every day except on Sundays and holidays. Daily routines began with an hour of prayer each morning. The rest of the day was spent performing the work needed to feed, clothe, and house all of the people at the mission. The men usually worked on buildings or in the fields. The women completed domestic chores, such as weaving and cooking. On Sundays, they would listen to the friars preach or read from the Bible.

Bells were rung to alert the Native people when it was time to wake, eat, work, and sleep. Little free time was allowed for games and relaxation—and even less was given for their former activities, such as hunting or traditional crafts that did not serve the missionaries.

Everyone at the mission ate *atole*, porridge made of corn. For dinner, there was *pozole*, a thick stew of corn, meat, wheat, peas, and beans. These meals were all made from food grown at the mission by the Native people. The foods were healthy and provided the people who lived at the mission energy to perform their tasks.

At Mission San Francisco Solano, the first project the neophytes completed was the construction of sleeping quarters for the soldiers and the friars. They then began working in the fields cutting down trees and preparing the soil for planting. To create an orchard, 160 fruit trees were planted. To make a vineyard, they put in 1,600 vines of purple grapes. The work was hard but deemed rewarding once the trees and grapes flourished. In addition to working in the fields, the neophytes tended the

Mission San Francisco Solano, shown here in a late nineteenth-century etching, housed more than 1,000 people at its peak.

horses and cattle that grazed in the pastures, fattened hogs in pens, and raised sheep for meat and wool.

There were other work-related projects as well. For weaving, Fray Altimira set up a large Spanish-style loom and taught the Native people, usually the women, to weave woolen cloth. They created carpets, blankets, and clothing. A blacksmith shop was also set up to make horseshoes, spurs, nails, and tools.

Raising cattle was especially profitable because of the trade in cattle hide and **tallow**. Tallow was made from cattle fat and used to make candles and soap. The gentle climate and rich grasslands of Alta California made it easy to raise cattle. Their hides then became known as "California bank notes" because they were in such abundance. By selling cattle hide and tallow, the missionaries were able to purchase manufactured goods from the United States, as well as Europe and Asia. Other items they bought were coffee, sugar, tobacco, farm tools, and fine decorations for the church.

Life at the mission was not easy.
Many neophytes were treated badly.
However, they often suffered even
greater hardship after they left.

FRUSTRATION AND ILLNESSES

Despite the many efforts to keep Mission San Francisco Solano running, life was not always happy or healthy for the people there. Fray Altimira and some of his missionaries were cruel to the neophytes. If the neophytes disobeyed, they would be punished by whippings or beatings. This led to many neophytes feeling depressed and unhappy; some even felt as if they were imprisoned. They missed their old ways of life, and wanted to leave the mission and return to their tribes. The friars, unfortunately, could not understand why the neophytes would feel this way. They thought everyone should live like the Spanish and would be happier if they did. Yet the Native people deserved to live the way they always had, not how the friars wanted them to live.

The Europeans did not just bring Christianity to the Natives—they also brought diseases. The Native population was not used to these new illnesses, including measles and smallpox, and as a result, had no immunities built up. While these diseases were not fatal to the Europeans, they were deadly to the neophytes. Large groups, up to 90 percent of the Native people, were lost within the first century of European colonization of California. These problems continued to affect Native people at each mission, including Mission San Francisco Solano.

7
Decline and Hardship

Because Fray Altimira treated the neophytes so badly, many attempted to escape from the mission. Soldiers were then sent out after them. Still, that did not stop people from leaving. A few made it back to their tribes and lived life as they had before the friars of Mission San Francisco Solano arrived.

Eventually, the neophytes who could not escape lost patience. In 1826, a large group of them attacked the mission. They looted, burned buildings, and damaged property and many important artifacts. They forced Fray José Altimira and the few neophytes who stood by him to flee for their lives. Not long after, Fray Altimira left Alta California and sailed back to Spain never to return.

UPRISINGS

That was not the end of conflicts between those who settled around the mission and the Native people. During the mid-1800s, Mexico went to war with Spain. The Mexican people wanted freedom from Spain's rule. Following in footsteps similar to those that sparked the American Revolution (1775–1783), many battles between Spain and Mexico took place. In 1821, Mexico finally gained its independence and took control of California. In the years after Mexico's revolt against Spain, uprisings from the neophytes continued. By the 1820s and 1830s, many groups of Native people were banding together and forming small armies, raiding the homes of ranchers who lived around the missions. They viewed the ranchers as "invading enemies" who had stolen their land. As a result, the ranchers were forced to take the raiders seriously. Sometimes they had to fight back with forces of 100 soldiers or more.

In addition to farming and Christianity, the Spanish had introduced the Native people to two important skills: the use of guns, and horseback riding. There were no horses in Alta California before the Spanish arrived. But once the Native people were taught to ride them, they became excellent horsemen. They also quickly learned how to use the weapons of the Spanish.

THE END OF THE MISSIONS

Soon after these raids, the California government passed laws to make it legal to kill Native males over the age of ten. The population of Native males was then drastically reduced. They were not the only ones to suffer, though. Women and children were often imprisoned in conditions that turned out to be fatal.

This was a tragic and horrifying end to the dream of the Franciscan friars. By 1823, when Fray José Altimira had reached the Valley of the Moon, it was probably already too late to build a mission. The land in California was unusually rich and people were willing to kill for its control. Greedy officials sold land to ranchers or gave it away illegally. The friars were not strong enough to change or confront these events. Because of disease

and warfare, the indigenous people were not strong enough to take back their land, and some turned to the mission system.

THE FRIARS OF THE MISSION

The man who replaced Fray Altimira as Mission San Francisco Solano's head friar was Fray Buenaventura Fortuni. Fray Fortuni was different from Fray Altimira, in that he treated the neophytes with respect. Hearing about the new friar, many neophytes who had left the mission out of disgust with Fray Altimira returned to welcome Fray Fortuni. Fray Fortuni remained at the mission from 1826 until his retirement in 1833. It was under his guidance that the mission reached the height of its success. In 1832, the mission experienced its highest population: 996 people. Over Fray Fortuni's seven-year tenure, the mission also grew to its largest size of thirty buildings, including a twenty-seven-room dwelling for the priests. Without doubt, Fray Fortuni's influence on the mission was a positive and prosperous one, and placed Mission San Francisco

This photograph of a painting shows Fort Vallejo and the original Mission San Francisco Solano c. 1900, after secularization.

Solano among the most successful of the twenty-one missions.

When Fray Fortuni left the mission, he was replaced by a Mexican friar, Fray José Gutierrez. Native people living at the mission strongly disliked Fray Gutierrez, who proved insensitive and cruel. It was then that Mission San Francisco Solano experienced another decline in its neophyte population. They feared Fray Gutierrez, like Fray Altimira, would treat them unfairly and cause them harm. Thus many left for other missions or vanished into the hills to rejoin their tribes.

Fray Gutierrez left Mission San Francisco Solano after a year and a half. His tenure was the shortest among all the California mission leaders. The next friar, Fray Lorenzo Quíjas, arrived just as the new Mexican government put an end to the mission system. As Mexico became its own country no longer ruled by Spain, their government controlled Alta California. They demanded that the missions be returned to the Native people, and that the Spanish priests leave. This process of closing the missions was called **secularization**.

8
Secularization

The Mexican government's ideas about what to do with the missions differed from those of the Spanish. They either wanted to remove the priests and send in other missionaries to continue the work the Spanish had started, or close the missions down completely. In 1833, the Mexican government passed laws to secularize the missions. This meant that the missions were no longer under the financial control of the Catholic Church, and that the neophytes were free to leave. Most of the Franciscan missionaries were sent back to Spain and replaced with priests who did not do missionary work.

DIVIDING THE MISSION LANDS

Many of the missions fell apart after secularization. A plan was made to divide the mission lands between the neophytes and the settlers. However, corrupt officials and greedy settlers discovered a way around this and took the land for themselves. Most of the lands at Mission San Francisco Solano were taken over in 1834 by Lieutenant Mariano Vallejo, a general who grew rich and powerful by working the mission land.

Secularization also had an effect on the mission's Native population. Some neophytes could not understand their freedom. Laws of ownership were foreign to them, so they did not understand how land could be taken from them. Also, life at the mission had changed them, and the thought of leaving it was frightening. For some, their Native villages no longer existed. Their ways of hunting and gathering were lost, and their rituals and languages forgotten. Their tribal leaders had either been killed or had gone into hiding. Their very culture had been lost, as well as their lands. This

General Mariano Vallejo (shown in the hand-colored woodcut above) took over Mission San Francisco Solano after secularization.

meant that their newfound freedom made their lives worse than they had been at the missions.

While many Natives returned to their villages, some remained behind to keep working at the mission. However, without the friars organizing the work and activities, many neophytes were unsuccessful and became homeless. These Natives were forced to work on local ranches or for General Vallejo. Others either became house servants or worked in local shops—jobs that did not pay well.

While for some secularization meant the end of Spanish ownership and rule, for others it completely changed their ways of life, and not always for the better.

Today the mission is known as Sonoma Mission and serves the community as a church, museum, and historical site.

9
The Mission Today

Mission San Francisco Solano closed its doors as a Spanish Franciscan mission in 1834. It was then managed by Mexican missionaries and General Vallejo. General Vallejo built a new church on its grounds in 1840, one much larger than the church Fray Altimira and the neophytes had constructed in 1823. It would serve as the parish for the town of Sonoma. In 1846, the mission witnessed the **Bear Flag Revolt**, which took place directly across from it. The event eventually led to California becoming a U.S. state in 1850. Sadly, Mission San Francisco Solano came to a temporary end in 1881, when the church and the friars' quarters were sold and used to store hay for thirty years. The church later became a blacksmith shop.

In 1903, the mission was deteriorating. Recognizing the importance the mission held in California's history, the California Landmarks League, a group dedicated to preserving historic sites, decided to save the mission. The league collected $13,000, purchased the mission, and then gave it to the state of California. In 1911, repairs began, and in October 1922, the mission opened as a museum. In 1943, it once again underwent restoration and reopened as Sonoma Mission, the name by which it is known today.

THE MISSION TODAY

Today Mission San Francisco Solano sits in the center of the town of Sonoma. Sonoma Plaza—the shaded square designed by General Mariano Vallejo—is surrounded by shops, restaurants, and historic adobe buildings. The old Mexican army barracks remain on the grounds along with some of the nineteenth-century hotels. The mission gives many tours throughout the year to visitors who are interested in the history of the Franciscan missions.

Sonoma, in the Valley of the Moon, is now best known as the birthplace of California wine making. Fray José Altimira planted the first grapes in Sonoma to make wine for Mass. Today Sonoma wines are enjoyed all over the world.

MODERN POMO AND COAST MIWOK PEOPLE

Although the Pomo and Coast Miwok people suffered greatly at the hands of the Europeans, their tribes have survived. Their traditions, burial and sacred places, and some of their land remain intact. The missions remaining today are reminders of the drastic lifestyle changes Native people endured. While Franciscan friars believed they were helping the indigenous people by bringing Christianity to them, the mission system threatened the Native people's existence, took their land, caused them suffering, and cost many of their lives. Ultimately, through all the hardship, they survived. Their storied history lives on in the stone buildings and wooden forts, the trees and fields that were there from the beginning, and the relics left behind.

10
Make Your Own Mission Model

To make your own model of Mission San Francisco Solano, you will need:

- bell
- cardboard
- fake flowers/trees
- Foam Core board
- glue
- green paint
- masking tape
- paint (white, brown)

- paintbrush
- pencil
- Popsicle sticks
- ruler
- sand
- scissors
- string
- X-ACTO® knife (ask for an adult's help)

DIRECTIONS

Adult supervision is suggested.

Step 1: Cut a square piece of Foam Core measuring 20" × 20" (50.8 × 50.8 centimeters) to use as the base of your mission. Paint the base green.

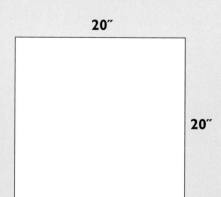

20″

20″

Step 2: Make the front and back of the large church by cutting out two cardboard pieces. Each should measure 8" (20.3 cm) in width, 9" (22.9 cm) high at the peak, and 8" (20.3 cm) high at the sides.

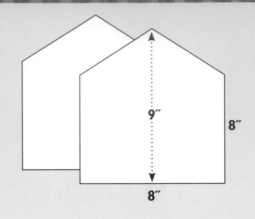

Step 3: Cut a door in the front of the church, and above it, cut a rectangle for a window.

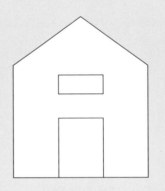

Step 4: Using the cardboard, cut two side walls that measure 8" × 8" (20.3 × 20.3 cm).

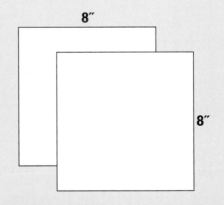

Step 5: Tape the front, back, and sides of the church together. Attach the mission church to the base.

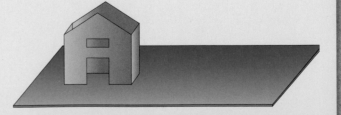

Step 6: Make two mission quadrangle walls that measure 5" × 4" (12.7 × 10.2 cm). Tape each so they stick out from the front and back of the mission church.

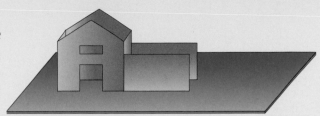

Step 7: To make the front and back of the small church, cut two pieces of cardboard that measure 4" (10.2 cm) wide × 7" (17.8 cm) high at the peak, and 6" (15.2 cm) high at the sides. Cut out doors and windows.

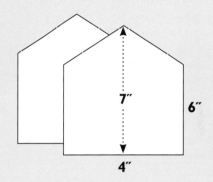

Step 8: Make two side walls for the small church that measure 8" × 6" (20.3 × 15.2 cm). Tape the front, back, and side walls together.

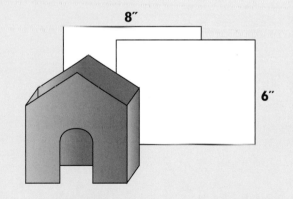

Step 9: Attach the small church and the quadrangle walls to the base. Mix sand and white paint together. Paint the mission with this mixture.

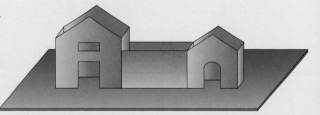

Step 10: To make the roof of the large church, cut out a 9" × 9" (22.9 × 22.9 cm) piece of cardboard and fold it in half.

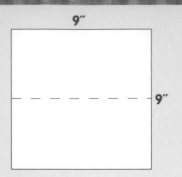

Step 11: Paint the roof brown and glue it to the top of the large church.

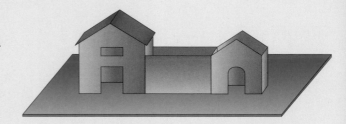

Step 12: Cut a 9" × 5" (22.9 × 12.7 cm) piece of cardboard for the small church roof. Fold it in half, lengthwise. Paint it, and then attach it to the small church.

Step 13: Break a Popsicle stick in half, lengthwise, and then into smaller pieces. Paint the pieces brown, and glue them above the church doors and windows.

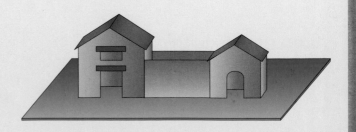

Step 14: To make the bell holder, cut 3 Popsicle sticks to measure 3" (7.6 cm) each. Paint them brown. Glue them together as shown and stick them into the Foam Core. Hang a bell with string or wire.

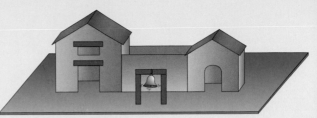

Step 15: Add trees and flowers to decorate the mission grounds.

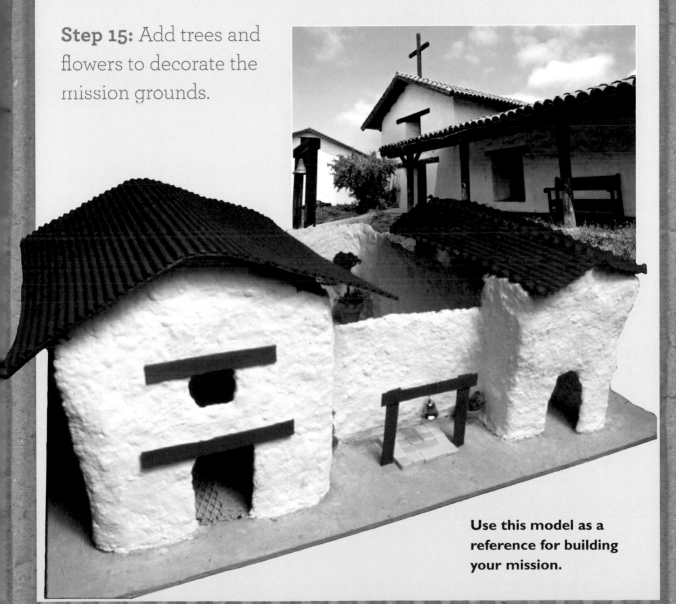

Use this model as a reference for building your mission.

Key Dates in Mission History

1492	Christopher Columbus reaches the West Indies
1542	Cabrillo's expedition to California
1602	Sebastián Vizcaíno sails to California
1713	Fray Junípero Serra is born
1769	Founding of San Diego de Alcalá
1770	Founding of San Carlos Borroméo del Río Carmelo
1771	Founding of San Antonio de Padua and San Gabriel Arcángel
1772	Founding of San Luis Obispo de Tolosa
1775–76	Founding of San Juan Capistrano
1776	Founding of San Francisco de Asís
1776	Declaration of Independence is signed

1777	Founding of Santa Clara de Asís
1782	Founding of San Buenaventura
1784	Fray Serra dies
1786	Founding of Santa Bárbara
1787	Founding of La Purísima Concepción
1791	Founding of Santa Cruz and Nuestra Señora de la Soledad
1797	Founding of San José, San Juan Bautista, San Miguel Arcángel, and San Fernando Rey de España
1798	Founding of San Luis Rey de Francia
1804	Founding of Santa Inés
1817	Founding of San Rafael Arcángel
1823	Founding of San Francisco Solano
1833	Mexico passes Secularization Act
1848	Gold found in northern California
1850	California becomes the thirty-first state

Glossary

adobe (uh-DOH-bee) Sun-dried bricks made of mud and straw.

Bear Flag Revolt (BEAR FLAG ri-VOLT) From June to July 1846, American settlers in Alta California staged a revolt claiming California as a republic, or its own country. The event, called "Bear Flag Revolt," took place across from Mission San Francisco Solano.

Christianity (kris-tee-ANN-ih-tee) A religious faith that accepts Jesus Christ as the Messiah, or Son of God.

convert (kuhn-VERT) To change religious beliefs.

cradleboard (CRAY-dul-bord) A baby carrier with a flat back, usually used by Native cultures in North America.

Franciscan (fran-SIS-kin) A member of a Catholic religious group started by Saint Francis of Assisi in 1209.

friar (FRY-er) A member of a men's Roman Catholic group who is poor and studies or teaches about Christianity.

granary (GRAY-nah-ree) A windowless building used for storing grain.

missionaries (MIH-shuhn-ayr-eez) People who teach their religion to others with different beliefs.

neophytes (NEE-oh-fyts) Native Americans who became Christians and lived at the missions.

quadrangle (QUAD-rain-gull) A geometric shape that resembles a square.

secularization (seh-kyoo-luh-rih-ZAY-shun) A process by which the mission lands were made to be nonreligious.

tallow (TAH-low) A solid substance made from cow or sheep fat. It is often used to create candles or soap.

tule (TOO-lee) Reeds used by Native Americans to make houses and boats.

viceroy (VICE-roy) A person sent by a king or queen to live in a foreign country and make decisions for the country, much like the king or queen would do.

Pronunciation Guide

atole (ah-TOH-lay)

El Camino Real (EL kah-MEE-noh RAY-al)

palizadas (pah-lee-ZAH-daz)

pozole (poh-SOH-lay)

Find Out More

To learn more about the California missions, check out these books and websites:

BOOKS

Gendell, Megan. *The Spanish Missions of California.*
New York, NY: Scholastic, 2010.

Kalman, Bobbie. *Life of the California Coast Nations.*
New York, NY: Crabtree Publications, 2004.

Weber, Francis J. *Blessed Fray Junípero Serra: An Outstanding California Hero.* Bowling Green, MO: Editions Du Signe, 2008.

White, Tekla. *San Francisco Bay Area Missions.* Minneapolis, MN: Lerner Publishing, 2008.

Williams, Jack S. *The Miwok of California.* New York, NY: Rosen Publishing, 2004.

WEBSITES

California Missions Foundation
www.californiamissionfoundation.org
Find quick and easy facts about the missions and discover more about the organization that preserves and protects the missions today.

California Missions Resource Center
www.missionscalifornia.com
Interact with a mission timeline, videos, and photo gallery and unlock key facts about each mission in the California mission system.

California State Parks: Office of Historic Preservation
www.ohp.parks.ca.gov
Discover what the Office of Historic Preservation is all about and how it helps parks such as the one in which Mission San Francisco Solano is located.

Index